Lollipop Brigade

The Wish

MYSTICAL MAGICAL 1

J.A. SWEENEY

ISBN 978-1-64468-027-8 (Paperback)
ISBN 978-1-64468-028-5 (Hardcover)
ISBN 978-1-64468-029-2 (Digital)

Covenant Books
11661 Hwy 707
Murrells Inlet, SC 29576
www.covenantbooks.com

These books are dedicated to all my bestest friends who have walked this journey with me. Who have believed in me from the very first moment and have cheered me on with each new adventure I've been on and each new character I have met. My cup of hearts overflows with glitzery love.

All of the characters that come alive through the vivid colors and visions, they are the real and caring children of the people that put their heart and soul into these stories. With each stroke of the brush, they come alive on the page and live through you. They are currently fulfilling these life lessons with their whole heart. May they bring sparkleness to the world like we know that they will.

And to each child and parent that embarks on these adventures with all of us, may you all bring happiness and glitzery thoughts to all of the people that come into your lives and live life like we do, making everyone you meet feel, BEAUTIFUL, SMART, COURAGEOUS, DARING and STRONG. Learn how to FORGIVE and have FRIENDSHIPS that will last FOREVER and ever, and always work together like FAMILY.

ALWAYS, always believe that you are the most AWESOME YOU and know that you SHINE like no other!

If you have found these lollipops, know that they will take you to magical places, on adventures that only you can imagine. Each lollipop has a power unlike the others. Each one is different and will take you to far away lands and mystical places. Keep the lollipops safe and locked away. There will be many magical adventures for you and many lands to visit. We hope you enjoy them as much as we did.
Your new friends,
Jen and Courtney

JOURNEY

v

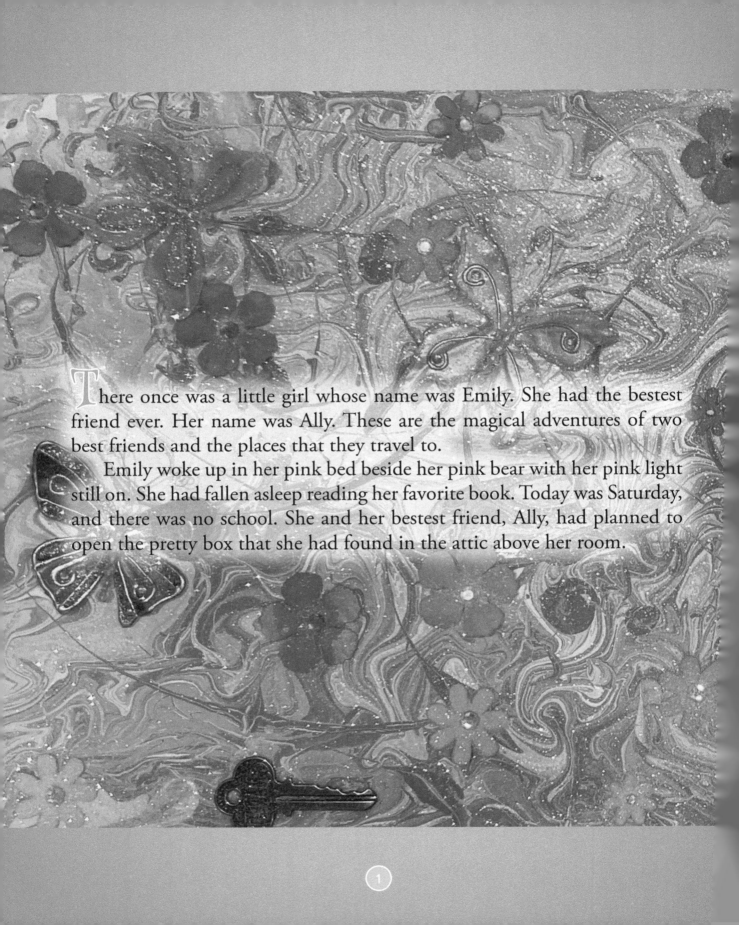

There once was a little girl whose name was Emily. She had the bestest friend ever. Her name was Ally. These are the magical adventures of two best friends and the places that they travel to.

Emily woke up in her pink bed beside her pink bear with her pink light still on. She had fallen asleep reading her favorite book. Today was Saturday, and there was no school. She and her bestest friend, Ally, had planned to open the pretty box that she had found in the attic above her room.

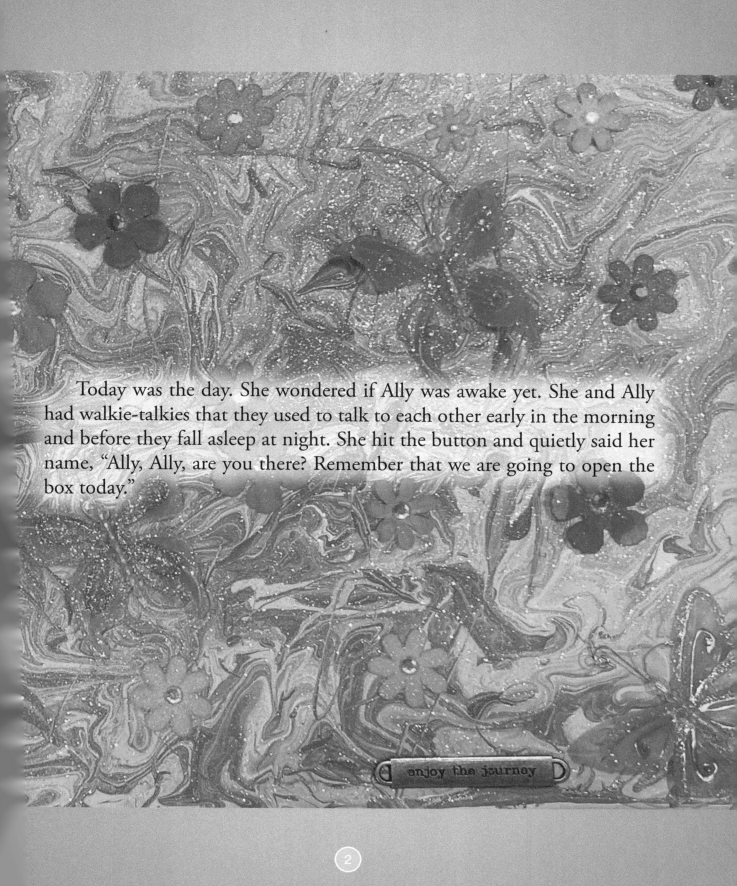

Today was the day. She wondered if Ally was awake yet. She and Ally had walkie-talkies that they used to talk to each other early in the morning and before they fall asleep at night. She hit the button and quietly said her name, "Ally, Ally, are you there? Remember that we are going to open the box today."

enjoy the journey

Just then the doorbell rang, and Emily jumped out of bed, ran downstairs, and threw open the door. It was Ally, and she had been waiting for Emily to call her.

"I'm here, I'm here, when are we opening it? When? When? Now?"

The girls ran up the stairs, jumping over the lazy dog that was still sleeping.

"Silly dog," said Emily.

"Lazy dog," said Ally, "she never does anything but sleep."

The girls ran into the bedroom and shut the door. They both ran for the bed and fell to the floor, reaching under the bed and then pulling out

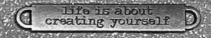
the pink box. It had a pretty lock on it, and they had found the key taped to the side.

They opened the door just to check that her little brother, Christopher, who Ally called Topher, was nowhere around. Seeing that the coast was clear, and the dog, Dixie, was still sleeping on the stairs, they closed the door and prepared themselves to open up the box.

They grabbed the key and swooped up the box and put them on the bed of pink lace. They both sat with their knees pulled up to their chest and looked at each other with excitement, wondering what was inside the pretty pink box. They put the key in the lock, turned it one time, heard the click, *and then…*the lock *opened.*

They both took a deep breath and flipped open the lid. To their surprise, inside the box were *lollipops*—lollipops with swirlies and some with sparkles and sprinkles, different colored ones and ones with pretty ribbons, and finally there was one with so many colors that they couldn't count them all.

Emily and Ally sat and wondered what to do, which lollipop to start with, and then wondered who put them in the attic. There must be something

special about them. They laid all of the lollipops on the bed—one, two, three, four, five, six…all the way to twelve. *Twelve* lollipops, but wait— there were two of each one. Now they wouldn't have to choose. They could each have matching lollies. That meant six each! They jumped off the bed, ran to the door again, and checked to see if that silly little brother was still in his room and that the dog, Dixie, was still sleeping on the stairs. Yep, everything was good.

dream as if you'll live forever

They closed the door and ran back to the bed and sat anxiously and talked about which one to unwrap first. Should they open the sparkly one? The ones with sprinkles, ribbons, or the one with so many colors that it looked like a rainbow?

"That one!" said Emily, pointing to the rainbow-looking lolly. "Let's open that one first."

They looked in the box, just to make sure that there were no more lollipops, but taped under the lid was a pink piece of paper.

"Do you think it's a letter?" Ally said. "Maybe it's a letter from the person who hid them in the attic."

the journey awakens the soul

They carefully took out the piece of paper, opened it, and read what it said, "If you have found these lollipops, know that they will take you to magical places, on adventures that only you can imagine. Each lollipop has a power unlike the others. Each one is different and will take you to faraway lands and mystical places.

Keep the lollipops safe and locked away. There will be many magical adventures for you and many lands to visit. We hope that you enjoy them as much as we did. Your new friends, Jen and Courtney."

The girls stopped and stared at each other with curiosity.

"What should we do?" asked Ally.

"I don't know" said Emily.

live the life
you've imagined

And then they thought and they thought and finally said at the same time, "Let's try one now!"

So they carefully unwrapped the one with colors like the rainbow. They looked at each other, held hands, and took their first lick. It felt like they were being transported through a kaleidoscope tunnel, filled with colors and swirls, and before they knew it, they were sitting on a bright-green patch of grass, where flowers dripped with sugar, and the bright-yellow sun was filled with lemon drop sparkles.

capture life's moments

11

They sat for a minute and looked around, taking in all that they were seeing. They looked at the flowers glistening with sugar in the sparkling lemon drop sun. They looked at the bright-green grass with the purple butterflies flying low in the orange-colored wind. A mountain of dandelions grew where red dragonflies were circling trying to catch all of the wishes that children had made.

Suddenly a small red dragonfly flew up beside Ally and landed on the wispy blade of green grass that laid beside her.

"Emily," Ally said, "She is looking right at me."

The dragonfly turned her head as though she understood and quietly said, "You are new here."

"New to where?" Emily asked. "Where are we?"

"You are in a magical land, where all of the creatures large and small fly. And now that you are here, you will fly too." Just then she flew away and yelled back, "My name is Dahlia. Follow me, and I will take you around the land."

possibility begins with imagination

So the girls stood up, put their arms up to the crimson-colored sky and let the orange-colored wind lift them away, following Dahlia and feeling the wind in their hair. As they flew above the bright-green grass, looking down at all of the cotton candy trees, they noticed that all of the land was as colorful as the lollipop that had brought them there.

know in your heart
you are loved

So colorful that they could not count all the colors. There were purple butterflies, blue bees, red dragonflies, pink birds, and aqua ladybugs! They followed Dahlia over the hills that were lined with chartreuse-colored daffodils where the red dragonflies had come after counting all of the wishes that children had made.

It was on this day that they met all of the butterflies, the bees, and more importantly the special dragonflies that answered all of the children's wishes. The girls knew that Dahlia had helped their wishes come true, and that every time they blew a wish from a magical dandelion in their front yard, *this* is where they came to be answered.

encourage your hopes,
not your fears

So when you are outside under the sparkling lemon drop sun with the snowflake white dandelions and you blow your wish, know that Dahlia and her red dragonfly friends are catching your wish and sending it back to you. And if you believe with all of the goodness in your heart, all of your wishes will come true.

10 Glitzery Deeds

_____
_____
_____
_____
_____
_____
_____
_____
_____
_____
_____
_____
_____
_____
_____
_____
_____
_____
_____
_____
_____
_____
_____

About the Author

J.A. Sweeney currently resides in California. Her positive outlook on life has prompted her to share this wonderful outlook with children and adults alike. Her love has truly been children and animals for as long as she can remember. This is her first of eighteen children's books, and she is currently working on a new series with upcoming child illustrators, once again believing that we should follow our dreams no matter what age. And she has always done her best to instill in everyone that they can be Beautiful, Smart, Courageous, Daring, and Strong. Learn how to forgive people and to have Friendships that last forever and ever. Friendships that will always be like Family.

CPSIA information can be obtained
at www.ICGtesting.com
Printed in the USA
LVHW011803050623
748920LV00006B/244